"Sacrifice"

A stronger state of mind,
I don't need a title.

My domineer is a product
of applying to the Bible.

Never had an idol.
Blessing after blessing.

I'm not entitled,
but they're spiteful.

God promised dominion
over ALL my rivals,

& Eternal Life.
Chance after chance,
I'm trying to get it right.

Because son of man is wicked.
If we had a chance,
we'd do it twice.

God calls it corruption.
Son of man calls it "A way of life."

Not everything is beneficial.
Soon we'll have to pay the price.

But that's why God gave us a gift.

4.   *67

We call him Jesus Christ.

To wash away our sins,
He was tortured
& gave his precious life.

To save our place in paradise.
We know the truth & see the light.

Call it what you want,
but that was the ultimate sacrifice.

"Addiction." (Explicit)

Live learn and forget.
I can list a million reasons
why I'm sad or upset.

Why I'm self-aware, insecure,
& wayyy out of check.

Why I'm still so depressed.
Why I have nothing left.

All this damn anxiety
is just a stupid topic.

A broad range of symptoms.
Medication in my pocket.

Down seven pills,
like it isn't toxic.

Weak-minded, self-doubting,
& a bit nostalgic.

But I'm observant.
Everybody tries to lecture me,
& tell me what's the best for me.

Wondering what kinds of secrets
everyone has kept from me.

Cause Alcohol and drugs kind of help,
but they mess with me.

7.   *67

So trust me I appreciate
whoever really checks for me.

Put my cellphone down,
because too many people's texting me.

Business or personal,
I can never let it pressure me.

3 am, still awake,
wondering what's next for me.

So I just take another pill
& let it take effect on me.

8.

"Adolescence." (Explicit)

See as a child,
I only opened up to a beat.

Ain't talk to nobody.
Shit, ain't nobody wanna talk to me.

Guess "antisocial" was an understatement.

Whether that's cliché or opinion,
I ain't care what other kids where saying.

Tried to smile at girls that passed me by,
but it's hard when you're kind of shy.

9. *67

Always walked away feeling stupid,
didn't know why.

Adderall in the morning.
Always went to school high.

Because socializing's always easier in
my mind.

Abnormal interest,
But idk, I guess that makes a guy a
geek.

Was never trendy.
Never had a checkmark on my sneaks.

10.   *67

Hypocritically if I had money, I had friends.

But I was always broke, so honestly it's a sad end.

Kind of is to this day.
Even though my saving's wayyyyy happier than it used to be back in the day.

I see some boobs then I get the urge to masterbate.

Then wipe it on my brother's shirt.
"Sibling powers, ACTIVATE!"

11.   *67

That nigga knew that now, he'd probably catch a case.

Wings on the Little Tikes car, like it's a wacky race.

Laughing at jokes, when I barely knew the reference.

Just another 12 hours in Juanito's adolescence.

"Mental Illness." (Explicit)

Self diagnostics.
I hate it.

Suicidal actions for attention?.
STOP FAKING!.

I want to end it real quick.
You don't comprehend the demons
that I deal with.

You want total sympathy,
when this is real shit.

I'm talking tears in my eyes.
I'm talking about the warfare that's
going on in my mind.

13.   *67

I'm talking 9 or 10 pills at a time.
I don't know if they're upset & I
don't know if they're fine.

Unfamiliar circumstance doesn't
give me butterflies.

It makes me fucking nauseous, & it
happens all the time.

Sometimes my only outlet is a pen.
So I'm begging you,

please stop treating mental illness
like it's a trend.

"Pros & Cons."

Okay. Yes my brain is big,
but my heart is even bigger.

& yes I have a temperament,
but only when it's triggered.

So try and tell me all my
imperfections.
I won't listen.

I decipher them myself.
It's irrelevant to list them.

From my perspective
it's just condescending criticism.

15.   *67

Although it may not be.
You're probably dropping wisdom.

My minds a bit chaotic
when I let it get to drifting.

Somehow I feel better
When there's something in my system.

At the same time I hate it.
I wake up and I'm tripping.

Off balance, crystal vision,
dysfunctional decisions.

16.   *67

I can go on & on
about what's wrong with Juan.

But let's focus on the pros,
& forget about the cons.

"What's wrong?" (Explicit)

What's wrong kid? Nothing much.
Emotions and such.

Sometimes I'd rather take a shot than
sit and smoke a dutch.

Now a lot of people thing its wrong,
but I don't give a fuck.

Healthy coping mechanisms?
Nah I'd rather stay stuck.

Because everyone's hurt.
Dealing with some sort of baggage.

18.

How the hell do I help you?
When I have my own damage.

My sudden waves of sadness.
My suicidal tantrums

It may sound a bit selfish,
but I'm only being candid.

I glorify the type of behavior
you find outlandish.

If you're odd then you're interesting,
so please raise your standards.

19.   *67

The softest hearts coming from the hardest parts of Camden.

But I suppose a single soul wouldn't understand it.

"The Pitts." (Explicit)

Survival of the fittest.
Better eat or be eaten.

In the trenches with some demons.
Black hearted, pure evil.

Disrespect them & they'll do you in.
Like that's a valid reason.

To be labeled "Real"
they would jeopardize their own freedom.

But I don't sell rocks.

21.   *67

I don't fear any man who bleeds,
nor a cop.

So put that gun down
& put your hands up. Let's rock.

Or would you rather not?
Are you really a man
or rather hide behind a glock?

"Balance."

I've done seen darker nights
brighter days.

Try to fight these crappy feelings.
They bombard me anyway.

& kick my ass up & down.
Insecurity getting loud.

& it's drowning out every sound,
as I fade away in the crowd.

Because I care way too much about
what people think.

23.   *67

A like or a follow would put the
biggest smile on my face.

Turn off my phone.
Put it down.

Take a walk
& I look around.

Then I don't feel so bad,
because it's a beautiful day.

www.ingramcontent.com/pod-product-compliance
Lightning Source LLC
Chambersburg PA
CBHW071917160426
42813CB00098B/547